FAMILY GUY™

BRIAN GRIFFIN'S GUIDE

to Booze, Broads, and the Lost Art of Being a Man

Helped into Print by **ANDREW GOLDBERG**

Based on the Series Created by **SETH MACFARLANE**

HARPER

NEW YORK · LONDON · TORONTO · SYDNEY

*To Lois, a great friend and
a remarkable woman
—B. G.*

*To Colleen, the love of
my life and a hot little
number in her own right
—A. G.*

HARPER

HarperCollins books may be purchased for educational, business, or sales promotional use. For information please write: Special Markets Department, HarperCollins Publishers, 10 East 53rd Street, New York, NY 10022.

FIRST EDITION

Designed by Timothy Shaner

Printed on acid-free paper

Library of Congress Cataloging-in-Publication Data
Goldberg, Andrew.
    Brian Griffin's guide to booze, broads, and the lost art of being a man / helped into print by
    Andrew Goldberg; based on the show [Family guy] created by Seth MacFarlane—1st ed.
        p. cm.
    ISBN-10: 0-06-089920-4
    ISBN-13: 978-0-06-089920-2
    1. Family guy (Television program). I. Family guy (Television program). II. Title.

PN1992.77.F27G66 2006
791.45'72—dc22   2006043656

06 07 08 09 10 ❖ 10 9 8 7 6 5 4 3 2 1

The views represented
in this book are not
the views of HarperCollins
Publishers. Nor are they the views
of the Fox Broadcasting Company.
They're my views, and I'm a dog,
so if anything I write offends you,
just whack me across the
nose with a newspaper.

Contents

Foreword

Dearest Reader,

h, my God. I can't believe you're actually thinking of taking lifestyle advice from the dog. **First off, Fido's a raging alcoholic.** He drinks like Charles Bukowski after a bad day at the post office. And he's not even one of those functioning alcoholics who manages to keep his addiction a secret, fools his friends, and eventually ascends to our nation's highest political office. No, he's the creepy letch who's sitting at the end of the bar at four-thirty on a Monday afternoon, muttering to himself about Scotch tape while ogling the waitress and not-so-furtively playing with his pud.

Second, he's a pervert. On more than one occasion I've wandered into the Fat Man and Lois's bedroom looking for a diaper or my copy of *Yertle the Turtle* only to find the esteemed author of this guide to "livin'" (by the way, Brian, that's not cute; learn how to spell, you douchebag) rooting through Lois's underwear drawer with his tongue hanging out. Now, I'm not sure if he was sweating or drool-ing—but either way, yech, double vomit, throw-up burp, and lingering acid reflux.

Finally, um, hello, he's a *dog*. He's afraid of vacuum cleaners, he uses his tongue as toilet paper, and, God is my witness, I once saw him eat a used tissue out of the garbage. And one can only hope that someone *blew their nose* with that tissue, because I've seen the Fat Man go MacGyver with a box of Kleenex once he's run out of Q-tips.

So, there you have it, reader. Drunk. Pervert. Eats people's earwax out of the garbage. But, by all means, read on. I'm sure the filthy mongrel has plenty to say.

Yours in prose,
Stewie Gilligan Griffin

> The ruptured capillaries in your nose belie the clarity of your wisdom.

introduction

t seems like somewhere between Dylan McKay and Clay Aiken, men forgot how to be men. It figures they need a dog to remind them. This is a guide to a life of style. A life of substance. In short, a life worth livin'.

Why, you may be asking yourself, should I take advice from a dog? The answer is that humans have failed you. Dr. Phil's homespun psychobabble is so simplistic it's ridiculous. And the guy's clearly got anger problems. It's like somebody mistakenly gave Chet, the class bully, a degree in psychology. The Fab Five (Carson, Kyan, Thom, Jai, and, uh, I don't know, Tito?) are also part of the problem, not part of the solution. And for the record, if Carson ever cuts up one of my T-shirts and sews the pieces onto the back of a denim jacket, I will grab him by the necktie he wears as a belt and beat the living fabulousness right out of him. I swear to God. And finally, while dude magazines, such as *Maxim* or *FHM*, are great for teaching you how to make a bong out of a grapefruit or convince a hooker to give you a freebie, at the end of the day their scope is limited. And is it me, or is *Maxim* rapidly running out of women to slather in gold body glitter and slap on their cover? I mean, last month it was the girl who calls the lottery on Univision, and I hear next month they're using Rhea Perlman.

So, I don't claim to have all the answers. I don't even claim to have most of them. I only claim to know more than the other jerks whom our culture's made rich seeking answers to fundamental questions such as "What should I wear?" "Whom should I date?" and "With a healthy diet and proper exercise, will I ever be able to lick my own taint?"—answers that our grandfathers' generation knew instinctually.

"I see London, I see France, I see Stewie's unsightly chapped ass."

"You ever stop and think, 'Wow, I'm married to that guy'?"

"Hey, Quagmire, isn't there an 'o' in 'country'?"

Family and Pals

The foundation of any real man begins with the people he lives with and the people he drinks with: his family and his friends. I hardly knew my real family (my father got run over by a milk truck when I was a puppy, and my mother put me up for adoption—or, rather, gave me away in a cardboard box lined with a dish towel), so I'll speak of my adopted family: the Griffins (Peter, Lois, Chris, Meg, and Stewie) and my Quahog pals (Quagmire, Cleveland, and Joe).

PETER

PETER IS A COMPLEX GUY. I know what you're thinking: how can a man who drinks his own bathwater be complex? Well, let me illustrate by exploring three negative and three positive qualities that Peter possesses.

In terms of his negative traits:

Number one: **Peter is fat.** How fat is he? He's so fat, he has his own orbit. To give you an idea of exactly how fat that is, John Goodman doesn't even have his

own gravitational pull. Peter is so fat, he could incubate an egg in the fold between his breast and his stomach. He's so fat, the last time he saw his penis it was with the aid of a two-ton hydraulic floor jack and periscope. Okay, enough shtick—I think you get the idea.

Number two: **Peter is stupid.** Over the years, we've seen many, many examples of Peter's stupidity: building a waterslide out of a staircase, selling his daughter into white slavery, purchasing volcano insurance, punching a pregnant woman, kidnapping the pope, inventing Crystal Pepsi . . . the list goes on and on. Suffice to say, he's picked his nose with a Phillips-head screwdriver a few too many times.

> Hey. If I'm fat, then Stewie's fat too, 'cause we wear the same size onesie.

Number three: **Peter is a borderline criminally negligent father.** I know Child Services has their hands full—what with kids being handcuffed to radiators and Courtney Love having a daughter—but they've really dropped the ball on this one. If I see Peter duct-tape Stewie to the grille of his car one more time ("Hey, Brian! Check it out! Wicked-cool hood ornament!"), I'm calling the hotline myself.

But he also has his positive traits:

Number one: **Peter is extremely generous.** When he took me in as a stray six years ago, I was *this* close to turning tricks for Asian businessmen under highway overpasses. Thankfully, Peter gave me a place to live, pays the cable bill, and even lets me sleep at the foot of his bed from time to time. And over the years, he's dealt with a lot of my crap—from biting him, to developing a nasty coke habit, to occasionally making clumsy, awkward passes at his wife—but his generosity has never wavered.

Number two: **If you ever get stranded on the ice world of Hoth, you can slice open Peter's abdomen and warm yourself in his innards.** (And you thought those things smelled bad on the *outside* . . .)

Number three: **Peter's a perfect drinking buddy.** He's always up for a boozer, he works in a brewery and isn't above stealing beer for his pals, and although he may be a little quick to pull the trigger on streaking, he's a lot of fun when he's loaded. Come to think of it, the last time he turned Stewie into a hood ornament, he was pretty wasted—and we all laughed our asses off.

So, when you take a step back, some of the very same attributes that make Peter a perfect drinking buddy also make him a borderline criminally negligent father. See what I mean? Complex.

BRIAN
Who the hell buys a novelty fire extinguisher?!

PETER
I'll tell ya who. Someone who cares enough about physical comedy to put his whole family at serious risk!

I did gagoogity that girl. I gashmoigitied her gaflavity with my googis.

QUAGMIRE

HOW TO DESCRIBE GLENN QUAGMIRE . . .

Hmm. Well, let me put it this way: You're waiting in line at a public restroom, and you've *really* gotta go. Finally, a free stall opens up, and Quagmire steps out. Trust me, pal: You'd better wait for the next stall. **They just don't make paper toilet-seat covers thick enough to repel whatever that guy's got.**

And his taste in women is nothing short of astounding: deep jagged scars, prosthetic limbs, eye patches, stomas, missing teeth, bullet holes, violent twitches, extra genitalia, stumps, squirters, homeless ladies, diabetics—he's like Caligula in a Hawaiian shirt.

And one final thing that always amazes me about Quagmire is the sheer intensity of his foot fetish. I mean, sure, every once in a while I see a pair of feet that turn me on (that Reese Witherspoon's got some nice feet), but Quagmire's in a whole different league. I mean, the guy can't walk past a Lady Foot Locker without going into an epileptic fit, shouting, "giggity," and grabbing his "googis." **There's a reason his photograph is posted in mall security offices all over Rhode Island.**

Tonight we're going to enjoy the smooth jazz of Charles Mingus, Norman Mailer is here to read an excerpt from his latest book, and then we also have a girl from Omaha who's hiding a banana. We'll find out where. Giggity-giggity. Giggity-goo.

CLEVELAND

BELIEVE IT OR NOT, CLEVELAND WAS A REAL SWINGING BROTHER back in the late seventies. He experimented with mind-expanding drugs and traveled the country in a conversion van emblazoned with his nickname, Hot Chocolate, while bedding-down nearly half a dozen white women—not to mention a Comanche waitress in Buffalo, New York. Oops, just got a note from my editor. Turns out they don't want me to call Cleveland a "brother." He was a real swinging African American gentleman. Anyway, what happened? **How did Cleveland lose his groove and turn so passive and domestic? In a word: Loretta.**

You know how every group of pals has that one guy who's married to or dating a complete bitch, and you all can't stand her, and, sure, maybe one of you in a moment of weakness has sex with her once or twice, but even that just goes another step toward proving the point that she's a no-good skank? Well, in our group, that was Cleveland and Loretta. And while I don't condone Quagmire sleeping with his best friend's wife, in the end it may have been just what Cleveland needed to start a new chapter in his life and, maybe just maybe, get his groove back.

Plus, now Loretta probably has gonorrhea, so that's good, too.

> Public urination is just wrong.

JOE

YES, JOE'S A HERO AND AN INSPIRATION AND ALL, but is it me, or is he trying just a little *too* hard with his whole macho, manly-man, testoster-one act? I mean, what's he compensating for? The fact that he can't walk? The fact that he's dead below the waist? (I mean, **I assume he can't achieve an erection. Although I'm not really sure how to verify that.** I definitely don't want to ask him, and I don't quite feel comfortable asking Bonnie. Perhaps Lois knows . . .) The fact that he can't climb a fence? The fact that when he's mingling at a cocktail party everyone in the room is automatically two heads taller than him? The fact that Elizabeth Berkley could be straddling his groin and thrashing about, like in that awesome pool scene in *Showgirls*, and he still couldn't feel a thing? Well, yeah, I guess he's probably compensating for all that stuff.

(By the way, I just spoke to Lois, and Joe cannot, in fact, achieve an erection. They had to retrieve his sperm through a process called electrostimulation in order to impregnate Bonnie. Science, huh?)

Shut up, maggot!

Why do you bring me here?!

I was gonna push those beds together and take you around the freakin' world, Brian. But a nice pat on the head is just as good.

LOIS

AH, LOIS. Lois is a fantastic woman. Compassionate, charming, attractive, and shapely, too. I mean, you can't tell in her normal tan pants and mint green shirt, but when she's wearing a tank top or an evening gown, or if you run into her on her way out of the bathroom after a shower, you can tell she's *very* well proportioned. And it's not just her physical appearance—I mean, a great set of cans is a great set of cans—but, there's an uncommon air of sensuality in everything she does, from folding the laundry to applying her makeup in a short, clingy robe.

Now, a lot of people confuse my ability to recognize Lois's many qualities as "having a thing for her." Nothing could be further from the truth, for the most part. Lois is my best friend's wife, and the two of us share a very special friendship that I wouldn't jeopardize for anything. Even if Peter gave me permission because I had saved his life or something. Or if he was debilitated by a terrible disease and could no longer perform sexually but still wanted Lois to experience the joys of a physical relationship. Or any other scenario one might think up involving a lot of booze, a *Three's Company*–style misunderstanding, or even Peter being lost at sea.

The point is, Lois and I are great friends. And that's all. Unless you've heard her say otherwise?

STEWIE

PEOPLE ARE ALWAYS ASKING ME, "IS STEWIE GAY?" And my standard answer is, "Not *yet*. But be patient."

Sure, the kid's only one year old. And he *has* fallen for a couple of women. But gayness is just over the horizon. I mean, what kind of toddler sits with his legs crossed? Or knows the full name and backstory of every character on *The O.C.*? Or sings "This Used to Be My Playground" into a hairbrush while parading around in

I've been a bawdy little monkey.

a pair of his mommy's high heels? Every time I look at the little diva, I can't help but think, "This is exactly what everyone thought about the kid from *Who's The Boss?* in 1987."

Another question people often ask is, "Why can *you* understand Stewie, but the rest of the family hears only gibberish?" I honestly don't know, but I can say that I envy their deafness, because the kid *never shuts up.* It's always, "Victory is mine!" or "Damn you all!" or "Look at my fanny!" It's enough to make you wanna sock him in the mouth, which I have done once. But before you judge me for hitting an infant, he asked me to do it so he could collect money from the tooth fairy. And I think the little deviant

enjoyed it, because afterward he asked me to spit on him and call him a slut.

At the end of the day, though, I must say the kid's kind of growing on me. Peter and the guys aren't the brightest crew in the world, and it's nice to occasionally have someone intelligent (albeit effete and maniacal) around with whom to discuss politics and see independent films (although if he makes me rent *Brokeback Mountain* one more time, I'm gonna freaking lose it—and I don't wanna ruin the ending for you, but Jake Gyllenhaal's the "catcher"). Also, there's a pretty good chance I may never have kids of my own (although I've had a few close calls), and I kind of like the idea of being a role model of sorts to the little squirt. Stewie would never admit it, but I've taught him a thing or two. Like how to mix a martini and how to smoke a cigarette. I never said I was a *good* role model. Just a role model.

> I'm just trying to fit in.

MEG

MEG, UH . . . MEG GETS A RAW DEAL. I mean, it's not like she's *that* bad. She has lots of positive qualities, like, um . . . well . . . she's punctual. Of course, she never really has anyplace to be or anything going on, so punctuality isn't exactly the greatest achievement. But she's also got a real solid trunk. I mean, try pushing that girl over. You can't. She's got a very thick base and a low center of gravity. She's like a Weeble. And, oh, picking her up after school is a good opportunity to scout the local high school talent. There are some sixteen-year-olds out there who look like they're at least twenty. Best to look but not touch. At least, that's my policy. Anyway, back to Meg. She's really pretty okay and, uh . . . Forget it, I can't do this. Meg's a train wreck.

She's a mouth breather. Which is not only annoying but also causes bad breath. I mean, this girl's halitosis is out of control. Lois and I actually did rock-paper-scissors one time to see who had to talk to her about it, and I lost. Wow. Talk about your awkward conversations. "Um, Meg, have you ever tried using Scope? Or dental floss? Or breathing through your damn nose?!"

You don't know anything about me.

Meg also has a spare tire and cankles, which, though not entirely her fault < that's Peter's genetic material flipping her the bird, right there>, are difficult to look at. And if you ever get stuck in a conversation with her, you just wanna blow your brains out. I'd honestly rather get neutered with a bread knife than spend an evening on the couch watching TV with her. The way I look at it, Meg's best shot in life is to work on her hot-saw skills and enter the Lumberjacks Challenge, thus taking advantage of her thick base. Because even the homeliest of those lumberjack ladies always seems to be married with like eight kids. And depending upon your sponsor, you can get free flannels and deer jerky.

CHRIS

ONE THING'S FOR SURE: THIS KID IS PETER'S SON. They're both large, slow, and exhibit highly questionable personal hygiene. I recently took a quick look under Chris's bed (now, *that's* dedicated journalism because the

• ADULT •
SUPERVISION
REQUIRED

place looks and smells like a bat cave) and found the following items: a weathered *Glamour* magazine from 2003, six or seven crusty socks, an open bag of Gardetto's Snack Mix, a handful of Kraft Singles wrappers, a half-eaten cork coaster, a Tara Reid nipple-slip picture (which I kept), and, when I looked up, about forty booger stalactites hanging from the bottom of his mattress. The whole scene was vaguely reminiscent of Kevin Spacey's apartment in *Se7en*.

Don't get me wrong. Chris is a sweet kid with a good heart, but there's clearly some mild brain damage or severe lead poisoning at work here. I once witnessed him carry on an entire conversation with a pita pocket, which culminated with him eating the snack while tearfully apologizing and screaming, "Oh, Khalid! What have I done?"

But Mother Nature's a mad scientist, and she compensated for Chris's tiny intellect and painful social awkwardness with a massive schlong. The kid truly has a Ferrari but no license to drive.

Finally, no discussion of Chris Griffin would be complete without touching on the Evil Monkey that he claims lives in his closet. Is it real? I have no idea. Chris certainly believes it's real, and his closet *does* smell like monkey droppings. But then again, Chris also believes in Spider-Man, the Easter bunny, and trickle-down economics. And the monkey droppings could just as easily be his own, because bladder control (along with hand-eye coordination and complex sentence structure) is not one of the kid's strong suits. So, I guess it remains a mystery . . .

FAMILY STORY

MOST OF YOU PROBABLY REMEMBER the time Jimmy Fallon deflowered Meg on national television and Peter proceeded to kick his smirking ass into next Tuesday. But what you *didn't* see is that Peter went on to beat up Chris Parnell, Maya Rudolph, and Fred Armisen, while Lois got into an extremely hot hair-pulling contest with Tina Fey, and I nearly got sexually assaulted by Darrell Hammond. The melee might still be going on had Rachel Dratch not appeared and pulled Chris Kattan out of one of her giant nostrils. He ate an apple like a monkey and acted horny and spastic, and all was forgiven.

"Hey, babe, just, uh, trying you again, listening to our guy Coltrane, you know it's— okay... uh, anyway, I got a fax earlier about cheap airfare to Cancún. Uh, I didn't know if that was you trying to reach me."

Broads

(And Why I'm Destined to Die Alone)

I JUST NEED A LEG TO HUMP!

It's no secret that I've had my ups and downs with women over the years. Girls, to be frank, confuse the hell out of me. One minute they want you to be strong and aloof, the next minute they want you to be vulnerable and sensitive. And God forbid you sniff one of their butts prematurely. (I'm not trying to toss your salad, okay, sweetheart? I'm just trying to learn a little bit about your genetics and see if maybe you're in heat. Get over yourself.)

Anyway, what follows in this next chapter is my best stab at understanding women. God help us all.

WHY I LOVE DAMES

THE WAY THEY SMELL. Whether it's the subtle hint of Ivory soap on a suburban housewife or the not-so-subtle fragrance of cheap perfume and peach body spray on a Las Vegas stripper, women smell great. Or at least better than men.

THEIR BOOBS. Okay, you got me—I'm a breast dog. I don't know what it is about boobs, and I can't go too far into detail or they won't sell my book at Wal-Mart, but there's nothing like staring at an ample rack while a woman's trying to hold a conversation with you.

THE WAY A CLASSY DAME FEELS ON YOUR ARM. Although, let's face it, if she's really hot and has nice breasts, you can make certain allowances in the class department.

THE WAY THEY LAUGH. With the obvious exception of Fran Drescher, a woman's laugh is like music to a man's ears. Especially if she's laughing at an only moderately funny joke, because then the song she's singin' is called "Keep Buyin' the Drinks, Cowboy, 'Cause You Might Have a Shot."

THAT CERTAIN, AS THE FRENCH PUT IT, JE NE SAIS QUOI. Which, loosely translated, means, "I don't know what." It's that indescribable, intangible, almost ethereal quality that true ladies possess. A certain charm, confidence, and femininity that defies the scope of normal, everyday language. Christopher Morley called it "the vibrations of beauty." I call it "not having a penis."

WHY I AM DESTINED TO DIE ALONE

SO, OF COURSE I LOVE WOMEN. But at the end of the day, they baffle me, and I always seem to find a way to screw things up. So much so that it's entirely possible (as Stewie reminds me every few days) that I could die alone and miserable, in an assisted-living retirement kennel in Fort Lauderdale.

First off, **my standards are too high.** For a dog who's about two and a half feet tall and doesn't even have his own place, I'm pretty particular. I need a woman with a body *and* a brain. And I always seem to find some little flaw in the good ones. Like this one girl—she was very pretty and she was a law student, but I couldn't get past her webbed toes. I mean, it wasn't like *all* her toes were webbed together like a Chernobyl villager's. But the fourth and fifth toes on her left foot had a bunch of extra skin that held them together, and, God, I don't even wanna talk about it . . . I think I'm gonna go throw up in the yard.

> I totally pooped on her carpet then vehemently denied it.

Okay, I'm back. Second, **I tend to sabotage relationships.** Whenever things are going well, I figure out a way to screw them up. Either I get scared and become evasive and aloof (like with the Chernobyl girl: I totally pooped on her carpet, then vehemently denied it. Talk about passive aggressive). Or I get too excited and try too hard to impress (like with this aerobics instructor I used to date: After only three weeks, I left a dead bird on her doorstep, which for a dog is like giving someone a diamond bracelet from Tiffany's. Do you have any idea how hard it is to catch a bird? Apparently, she thought it was too much too fast, because she cried and made me throw it in the dumpster).

Finally, because I've been burned so often in the past, **I have trouble letting my guard down and being myself.** I get nervous around girls I like, and I tend to hide behind lame jokes and lots of booze. In fact, just talking about it is making me kind of thirsty. Let's see what Peter's got in the old liquor cabinet.

Helloooo, Jack Daniel's . . . .

THE ONES THAT GOT AWAY

NOTHING LIKE A GLASS OF JACK to make you nostalgic for old girl-friends, huh? So, while my buzz is mounting, let's take a look back at some of the babes (and bitches) who got away.

SEA BREEZE (CARTER PEWTERSCHMIDT'S PRIZE-WINNING RACE-DOG): I don't usually go for canines, but I met Sea Breeze at a time when I was suffering from a little "doggie fever" (Lois even caught me huddled in the bathroom with a copy of *Kinky Canine Coeds*). Plus, if you had felt the heat coming from that dog's genitalia, I doubt you would have been able to control yourself either.

WHAT WENT WRONG: Giving new meaning the word "bitch," it turned out Sea Breeze was two-timing me with Ted Turner.

PEARL BURTON (OLD-TIME COMMERCIAL JINGLE SINGER AND ILL-TEMPERED OCTO-GENARIAN): Pearl wasn't my usual type either. She was cranky, bitter, osteoporotic,

and had breasts that hung like wet tube socks filled with quarters. But she also had a beautiful singing voice, and once I coaxed her out of her shell, an inspiring zest for life.

WHAT WENT WRONG: As soon as I convinced her to leave her house for the first time in thirty years, she was run over by a moving truck. Love sure can be a bastard.

BROOKE ROBERTS (ASPIRING ACTRESS, BACHELORETTE CONTESTANT, AND MAJOR-LEAGUE HOTTIE): Brooke was something else. She was gorgeous, well built, witty, knew her jazz, and, my lord, when she kissed me, I thought my tail would never stop wagging.

WHAT WENT WRONG: She broke my heart on a national TV show and dodged my increasingly pathetic phone calls for more than three weeks. In the end, though, I was able to incorporate some of that heartbreak into my novel. Which I'm still working on.

SHAUNA PARKS (MEG'S HISTORY TEACHER AND PART-TIME CIVIL RIGHTS ACTIVIST): Shauna was also beautiful, but she had a little more depth than Brooke, plus a bigger bootie. Now, I don't mention that because Shauna's black—er—African American. I mean, a bootie's a bootie, and Shauna's was larger than Brooke's. So, relax. Although, in retrospect, I don't know why I brought it up in the first place. Can we cut this part? No? We need it for the page count? Damn.

WHAT WENT WRONG: Shauna tried to make me choose between her and Peter. And I believe it was Obi-Wan Kenobi who said, "Bros before hos."

GUEST ESSAY: STEWIE

THE BEST WAY TO INDUCE VOMITING UNTIL YOUR EYES WATER AND YOUR NADS ACHE? WATCH THE DOG FLIRT.

Pathetic. Hapless. Feeble. Stomach churning. Repugnant. Nauseating. Malodorous. Those are the words that come to mind when I think of the dog flirting. Here, allow me to break down the pitiful process for you:

First, he debates for fifteen minutes whether or not he should approach the unfortunate, unwitting girl. "Should I go? What if she hates me? What if she thinks I'm not tall enough? No, I'll go. I'm gonna do it. Is my breath okay?" Of course not, you filthy mutt! You lick your own poop chute!

Then, when Brian ultimately does decide to approach her, he begins to "psych himself up." "Don't worry, man. You're cool. You're good with chicks. Of course she'll like you. You've dated women much hotter than her. You know jazz. You're cultured. You used to write for *The New Yorker*." This is the first time I vomit.

Next, Hooch (or is it Turner?) wipes his sweaty paws on his fur and walks over to the poor woman. At this point, the verbal diarrhea begins to flow. "Wow, uh, that's, uh, that's a lovely dress. I mean, er, you're lovely, um, in the dress. Duh, I'm Brian, and I'm, uh, a total babbling half-wit!" **Oh, and, don't ask me how it's even possible for a creature**

who doesn't wear a shirt to get pit stains, but somehow Rover the walking, talking sweat gland makes the impossible a reality.

Next come the sad little jokes. "Hey, so you're a stewardess, huh? Bet you're glad to have a drink that doesn't come off a rolling cart." I vomit again.

Finally, the rejection. Either she doesn't give out her phone number, or she's got a pretend boyfriend, or sometimes—and this one's my favorite—she just got out of a really difficult relationship, and he seems like a nice guy, but she's just not ready to meet somebody new. Then (and this is the really spectacular part) she turns around and starts sucking face with some greaseball on the next stool who's wearing a leather jacket and a pinky ring. Ha!

In the end, Brian morosely returns and makes up some pathetic excuse like, "Eh, she's stuck-up" or "Eh, she's a lesbian." And then, if there's anything at all left in my intestines, I puke once more, right on his feet. Not because I have to, but purely to add insult to injury.

So, ladies, a word of advice: if you're ever camped out in some sleaze-pit bar, and Cirrhosis the Wonder Dog starts staring at you and wagging his tail, run as fast and as far as you can in the opposite direction, and never look back. Because, as the title of this little essay suggests, when I regurgitate repeatedly my testicles begin to ache, and I don't want that to happen. And I'm pretty sure you don't either.

Best wishes, SGG

MUTANT!

QUADRUPED!

TOP FIVE OVERLOOKED HOTTIES

GLENN CLOSE. She is a very handsome woman. In fact, I have no idea what Michael Douglas was thinking at the end of *Fatal Attraction*. I would have totally picked Glenn Close over Anne Archer. I mean, with dementia like that, you know the sex has gotta be pretty wild.

OLYMPIA DUKAKIS. Tough, worldly-wise, and almost regal. Plus, I love all that extra skin around her neck.

ASIAN REPORTER TRICIA TAKANAWA. She's erudite, has a professional yet sensual voice, and thanks to Pearl Cream, has a smooth, velvety complexion. Plus, I've got a sneaking suspicion that beneath her conservative skirt suit lies a wanton, Far East hellcat.

BJÖRK. Umlauts are sexy.

GEENA DAVIS. Nah, I'm just kidding. She looks a little too much like Jeff Goldblum for my taste.

THERE AREN'T ENOUGH CONDOMS IN THE WORLD

CHRISTINA AGUILERA. I feel like if I "rubbed her the right way," I'd get a rash.

PARIS HILTON. I heard that the car she was washing in that Carl's Jr. commercial is suing her for sexual assault.

JAIME PRESSLY. What an amazing actress. She's very convincing as low-rent white trash on *My Name Is Earl*. *Very convincing.*

ELIZABETH HURLEY. Someone told me that after you're done pleasuring her, she makes you watch *Bedazzled* three times in a row without bathroom breaks. That's why Hugh Grant got caught trying to have sex with that enormous hooker who looks like Big Shirley from *What's Happening!!*

KATIE HOLMES. On second thought, I have nothing bad to say about Katie Holmes. So, please, nobody ruin my credit or throw me into the back of an unmarked van. Thanks.

GAL STORY

I'M NOT SURE what would have happened with me and Pearl had she not been run over by that moving truck. I often wonder how we would have worked out the whole "physical" thing. I mean, I don't mind a mature woman, but she had more liver spots than Estelle Getty and a lot of loose skin. On the plus side, though, I wouldn't have had to use any "protection," because her ovaries dried out decades ago.

Chapt

"Me, I like the sauce."

"Hey, barkeep, whose leg do you have to hump to get a dry martini around here?"

"There, now if I can just find a midget with some gin, I'll be in business."

Booze

(Living Large and Lubricated)

A MARTINI A DAY KEEPS THE FLEAS AWAY

This I *am* an expert on. It's true, I like the sauce. Some say I drink to overcome feelings of abandonment from my childhood. Others say it's to numb the disappointment of being a nobody and accomplishing very little with my life. Still others say it's an allegory about the duality of man's mind versus his animal nature. All of you people need to shut the hell up and get a life.

WHY I HIT THE BOTTLE

My reasons are threefold:

LIQUID COURAGE. I sometimes feel a little, well, anxious in social situations, especially with members of the opposite sex. I think this is justified, given that I stand two and a half feet tall, have a retractable penis, and can't hear a high-pitched whistle without losing control of my central nervous system. A few drinks often help me overcome that initial apprehension and really be myself. A few more drinks often turn me into Pat O'Brien.

LIQUID THERAPY. Frank Sinatra used to say, "I'm for anything that gets you through the night, be it prayer, tranquilizers, or a bottle of Jack Daniel's." Well, I'm an atheist, I don't do so well with pills, and a bottle of booze is a lot cheaper than therapy. Although, if you get cirrhosis, the costs start to even out.

WHEN YOU'VE HAD A HANDLE OF JACK, EVERY WOMAN LOOKS LIKE AVA GARDNER. Let's face it, most people out there are ugly. Too ugly to date. You don't believe me? Head down to your local post office some lunchtime and tell me what percentage of the people in line you'd have sex with sober. "Beer goggles" or "gin glasses" or "absinthe binoculars" or whatever the heck you wanna call them, perpetuate the species and keep portly women from being lonely.

> Those are huge. Those are huge boobs. And you know what's nice? They don't have that blue vein up there that some of the bigger ones get.

> Shaken, not stirred.

49

MY FAVORITE SPIRITS
(THE LIQUID KIND)

AS THE LEGEND GOES, one night back in the early forties, a young Frank Sinatra turned to Jackie Gleason and said, "I wanna get smashed. Now, what's a good drink?" Gleason, shocked to learn that Frank had never gotten smashed before, shouted back, "Jack Daniel's! That's a good place to start!" By the end of the decade, Frank was drinking a bottle of Jack every night and traveling with ten cases in the cargo hold of his private jet. **If it was good enough for Gleason and Sinatra, it's good enough for me.**

Jack Daniel's is a great late-night drink, and there's nothing like a little brown liquor when you wanna start some trouble, but for the daytime (or early evening) or more civilized moments, I prefer a nice straight-up, very dry martini in an iced glass. It's a civilized drink for a civilized mammal.

A Bloody Mary is a great early-afternoon eye-opener. And if you've suffered any cuts or scrapes from the night before (most likely the Jack is at least partly to blame) you can just pour any extra vodka right over them. It'll sting for a few minutes, but it's better than peroxide, and as soon as you finish that Bloody Mary, you'll feel a whole lot better.

Finally, in recent years, I've become a bit of a sucker for a nice, refreshing mojito. And no, I don't think it's a gay drink.

THE LOST ART OF THE TOAST

OUR GRANDFATHERS' GENERATION knew how to toast. It didn't have to be a special occasion. It didn't have to be a fancy affair. Just a simple, elegant, thoughtful toast at a neighborhood watering hole. Nowadays, it's a minor miracle if a bunch of frat boys offer so much as a "bottoms up" before tossing back their Jager shots. So, with that in mind, I urge you readers (if, of course, you're of legal

drinking age) to toast when you drink, to choose your words wisely, and to switch up your toast every few months, so the ritual doesn't become stale.

And to give you a little inspiration, here are some of my favorite toasts from the past sixty-plus years:

FRANK SINATRA: "Here's to the confusion of our enemies!"

COSMO KRAMER: "Here's to feeling good all the time."

WINSTON CHURCHILL: "To Premier Stalin, whose foreign policy manifests a desire for peace. A piece of Poland, a piece of Hungary, a piece of Romania . . ."

JUDGE SMAILS FROM *CADDYSHACK*: "It's easy to grin when your ship comes in and you've got the stock market beat, but the man worthwhile is the man who can smile when his shorts are too tight in the seat."

GREGORY PECK IN *THE WORLD IN HIS ARMS*: "Here's to girls and gunpowder!"

GROUCHO MARX: "I drink to your charm, your beauty, and your brains—which gives you a rough idea of how hard up I am for a drink."

THE DANGERS OF DRINKING
(OR SIX MOMENTS I SWORE I'D NEVER DRINK AGAIN)

DECEMBER 12, 2000: Woke up on a tramp steamer headed to Portugal with Santos and Pasqual.

AUGUST 21, 2001: Asked Tony Danza to tell me, in detail, what it was like being a boxer.

JANUARY 4, 2003: Passed out midcoitus with a throw pillow.

APRIL 19, 2003: Ran over a homeless guy.

SEPTEMBER 8, 2004: Mounted a border collie who did not have her shots.

NOVEMBER 12, 2005: After an all-night bender with Peter, accidentally made a pass at Chris. Although, to be fair, I had just seen *North Country*, and I thought he was Charlize Theron.

HOOCH STORY

ONE NIGHT, I WAS EXTRAVAGANTLY DRUNK, and I was peeing on the fire hydrant out on Spooner Street. Well, Joe wheeled out of his house, with a full head of steam, and started writing me citations for indecent exposure *and* drunk and disorderly conduct. And I was like, "Joe. I'm a dog! I pee on this fire hydrant every single day! It's like my toilet." But I guess I swung around a little too quickly, because I peed all over Joe's leg. Fortunately, he's a paraplegic, so he didn't feel a thing.

"No thanks. I've been to New York. It's like Prague sans the whimsy."

"Kid, you're talkin' to a guy who uses his tongue for toilet paper."

"If you're gonna pull a party out of your ass, you might want to stand up."

Style

(The Way You Lick Your Balls)

Style is the business of comporting one-self. It's how you dress. It's where you hang out. It's how you behave. It's the unique verve and panache you bring along with you every time you enter a room. George Clooney, for instance, has a well-coiffed, throwback, man's-man style. Jon Stewart has a self-deprecating, intelligent, every Jewish mother-in-law's dream come true style. And Joaquin Phoenix, well . . . he has no style (unless you count sanctimonious veganism as panache).

METROSEXUALITY

IF FRANK SINATRA WERE ALIVE TODAY, he'd flatten Ben Affleck, Ryan Seacrest, David Beckham, and Justin Timberlake with a right hook to their pretty chops. Seriously, when exactly did male style consciousness become synonymous with narcissism and excessive vanity? It used to be that stylish men would drink whiskey, wear dark suits, smoke cigars, swing hammers, drive Cadillacs, and occasionally kick the living crap out of each other at neighborhood saloons. Now stylish men (or "metrosexuals") drink saketinis, wear couture (not clothing), manscape, drive chili red Mini Coopers, get pedicures, smell like berries, and care very deeply about exfoliation. I swear, some of these guys are half a step away from ovulating.

> I leave more personality in tightly coiled piles on the lawn.

Which brings me to my next point: there's a fine, fine line between "metrosexuality" and "just plain gay." Allow me to illustrate through a comparative chart:

	Heterosexual	Metrosexual	Homosexual
Prototype	Humphrey Bogart	David Beckham	Elton John
Worst-Case Scenario	Joe Rogan	Ryan Seacrest	Mario Cantone
Favorite Pastime	Football	Shopping	Sodomy
Worst Nightmare	Sodomy	Crow's-feet	President Jeb Bush
Favorite "Friend"	Jennifer Aniston	David Schwimmer	Lisa Kudrow
Dream Job	Astronaut	Record producer	Closeted actor
Dream Wife	Jennifer Garner	Lizzie Grubman	Ben Affleck

In conclusion, what I'm calling for is a return to the classic masculine style exemplified by the icons of our grandfathers' generation: Cary Grant, Humphrey Bogart, Steve McQueen, Dean Martin, and, yes, Frank Sinatra. Those guys parted their hair meticulously and wore sharp suits, but they weren't afraid to break a fingernail or damage their cuticles punching some schlub in the face. And they'd drop dead before being caught with Ryan Seacrest's frosted tips, Ben Affleck's L'Oréal face cream, or Justin Timberlake's overblown sense of self-accomplishment (not to mention his metallic blue toenail polish).

THE PERFECT BAR
(OR WHY MODERN NIGHTCLUBS SUCK ASS)

PETER RECENTLY DRAGGED US to a new nightclub called The Hot Spot. He wanted to find a new woman for Cleveland and someone to sit on Quagmire's face. Have you been to one of these clubs recently? They're miserable. Loud, crowded, overpriced, jammed with Tara Reid clones and Euro-jackasses in leather pants, and it takes about forty-five minutes to order a drink.

What's a gentleman's idea of the perfect bar? Well, first of all, it's quiet enough that you cannot only hear yourself think, but you can also carry on a conversation with your pals or the young lady you're entertaining. Second, there's beer on tap,

not just in bottles. Even if you're not drinking beer that night, it's nice to know that somewhere under the bar are several large vats filled with alcohol. Next, there should be some type of music—a jukebox or even better, a piano. Finally, the perfect bar should have a favorable gals-to-guys ratio. Because **nobody wants to spend a night in a sausage factory. Not even a dog.**

MEN HAVE FORGOTTEN HOW TO DRESS

NOT THAT i USUALLY WEAR

MUCH aside from a red collar and brass tag, but still (at the risk of sounding like Andy Rooney or Bill Cosby), kids today need to be reminded how to dress.

First of all, **pull up your pants.** Back in the day, they had a name for a guy whose pants were falling down, and it was "hobo." And they used to give him a piece of rope to

Pull up your pants!

wear as a belt (or in more extreme cases, a large, wooden barrel with suspenders to wear instead of pants).

Second, your faux vintage T-shirts aren't attractive or funny. They're ratty, embarrassing, and stupid. "Everyone Loves A Jewish Boy"? Not Louis Farrakhan. "Wiffle Ball Legend"? Try "Adult Virgin." And "The Butterscotch Stallion"? Really? You really wanna walk around with a picture of Owen Wilson on your chest? *Really*?

And, finally, whatever happened to a nice, sharp, two-button suit? If it's not Bono in a New Age black-on-black "I'm from the future where everyone dresses like an android priest" ensemble, it's Kevin Federline in a rumpled sports jacket, a mustard-stained T-shirt, and camouflage cargo pants. And by the way, Kevin: you're not fooling anyone with that camouflage. We can all still see you. Although, at least one of us—me—wishes to God he couldn't.

As far as the ladies go, some critics have argued that admiration of celebrisluts like Britney Spears and Paris Hilton has caused teenage girls to dress too promiscuously. I say pass the remote control, because I'm watching *Laguna Beach*. (On mute, of course.)

SWINGIN' STORY

A LITTLE WHILE BACK, I did a lounge act with Frank Sinatra Jr. and Stewie. And although I eventually blew the deal due to some heavy drinking, I did manage to glean a little Sinatra-esque wisdom before we parted ways. For instance, one time, I was a flirting with a girl backstage, and I gave her my hotel room key. Frank pointed out that I'd made a real amateur faux pas, because what if I went on to meet a more attractive young lady later in the evening? I should have just given the original girl my room *number*. Because then, if she knocked at 1:00 A.M. and I was otherwise engaged, I could dismiss her to my guest as a psychotic or an overzealous groupie.

There's a reason they called frank's dad the "Chairman of the Board."

"Maybe you can cut the whole chevy chase thing. Seems like he's probably the kind of guy who might sue. I mean, the guy's gotta have no money left."

Entertainment

(Music, Movies, and the Warm, Glowing Box That Peter French-Kisses Sometimes When He Thinks No One Is Looking)

You're gonna find that my "they don't make 'em like they used to" attitude carries over into the world of music and film. It's not that there haven't been a few good movies and albums over the past decade or so (*Hotel Rwanda*, *City of God*, *Marsalis Standard Time, Volume 1*), but the classics are classics for a reason.

MUSIC
(WHY EVERY SONG RECORDED AFTER 1972 BLOWS)

THE RECORDINGS of yesteryear (Sinatra, Bing Crosby, Henry Mancini) were lush, textured pieces of art, with large, virtuosic bands and a sense of style and grandeur. Today, we have crap like "Trapped in the Closet" and "My Humps."

Below are the five contemporary "artists" whom I personally find most offensive:

ASHLEE SIMPSON: You know you suck when *Jessica's* the "talented sister."

COLDPLAY: They have money, fame, and women. Why are these a-holes so sad?

JAMIE FOXX: Remember how after *Ray* he kept telling people that he *was* Ray Charles? How come after *Stealth* he didn't tell anyone that he *was* a military airplane that through a freak lightning accident somehow achieved human-style intelligence?

USHER: Come on, man. Put on your damn shirt. Seriously.

KEVIN FEDERLINE: You know you're dealing with a special performer when you don't even need to hear his music to know that he's awful.

MOVIES
(THEY DON'T MAKE THESE LIKE THEY USED TO EITHER)

> They don't make these like they used to either.

RATHER THAN MAKE A LONG LIST of all the terrible movies that were released over the past decade, I thought it would be easier to simply track the career of one popular actor who I feel best embodies everything that's gone wrong in Hollywood since Jay met Silent Bob. And who better than America's favorite smirking pretty boy and semicompetent thespian, Ben Affleck? His celebrity so far outshines his talent, he makes Joe Isuzu look like Albert Finney.

JULY 1998: *ARMAGEDDON* In this apocalyptic train wreck, Affleck flexes his "action star" muscles while also showcasing his sensitive side in the infamous animal cracker scene, where he debates whether or not the tasty snacks are, in fact, crackers or, rather, cookies. Those of us in the audience choose to debate the far more provocative question of whether Ben is, in fact, a jackass or, rather, a tool.

MARCH 1999: *FORCES OF NATURE* Here we are introduced to Ben Affleck the Smug Romantic Comedy Guy. He is equally as irritating as Ben Affleck the Action Pinhead, but a slightly lower box-office draw. Affleck is also paired with Sandra Bullock (*Two Weeks Notice, The Lake House, Miss Congeniality 2: Armed and Fabulous*) in this one, which is like a perfect storm of movie suckiness.

MAY 2001: *PEARL HARBOR* The studio reportedly paid Affleck twelve million dollars to be in this movie. Couldn't they have found something better to do with the money? Like, I don't know, dump it in a river? Or light it on fire? My favorite part of the film, though, would have to be Big Ben's reaction when he figures out that Kate Beckinsale and Josh Hartnett are a couple; he looks like a chimpanzee slowly discovering that the reflection in the watering hole is actually him.

AUGUST 2001: *JAY AND SILENT BOB STRIKE BACK* It's like Kevin Smith said to himself, "How can I possibly make this self-indulgent fiasco worse than it already is? I know! I'll have my buddy Ben Affleck play a character in the movie *and also* play himself! But, wait. . . . How will people tell Ben Affleck the character from Ben Affleck the jerky movie star? I've got it! The character will have a goatee! Eureka! Perfect! I don't care what anyone says about the second half of *Chasing Amy*, I am a goddamn genius!" By the way, around this time, rumors started circulating that

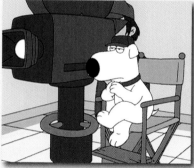

Ben Affleck wears a wig, which, if true, is just fantastic.

AUGUST 2003: *GIGLI* The birth of the two-headed, nineteen-toed monster known as "Bennifer." Stephen Hunter of the *Washington Post* wrote this of the movie: "Ach. Oy. Woe and poo, bleccch and uck! ZZZZZ-zzz." I'm not kidding. He really wrote that in a freaking newspaper. How could it get any worse?

MARCH 2004: *JERSEY GIRL* More Bennifer. More Kevin Smith. More awkward, misfiring jokes. More sappy, immature sentimentality. And more groaning from a certain dog sitting in the back row of the movie theater who only bought the ticket because he thought he'd get to see some J-Lo boob.

Coming up, Affleck is appearing in *Smokin' Aces*. I can't wait to not see it.

GUEST ESSAY: Peter

Kristy McNichol, come back to television. We miss you.

THE WARM GLOWING BOX THAT I FRENCH-KISS SOMETIMES WHEN I THINK NO ONE IS LOOKING

It's true. Late at night, after all the kids have gone to bed and Lois has fallen asleep, I go downstairs and tongue-kiss the television set. Why? Because I'm really freakin' wasted. And because I love TV.

In fact, by the power of Grayskull, here are my ten favorite TV shows of all time:

Dear MacGyver, enclosed is a rubber band, a paper clip, and a drinking straw. Please save my dog.

Happy Days: The Fonz was so cool, it didn't even matter that he failed his GED four times and lived in a one-room apartment over the Cunninghams' garage. He still managed to get into Pinky Tuscadero's pants every other season.

Airwolf: It's a freakin' *wolf* in the *air*. Come on!

MacGyver: He could make gazpacho out of a paperclip, three tomatoes, an onion, a cup of lemon juice, and a Cuisinart.

The Facts of Life: Although I still can't believe Natalie was the first one to lose her virginity. I always thought it would be Mrs. Garrett.

St. Elsewhere: A little bit of trivia: not a real Saint. But still, a great show.

Bernie Mac: I love it when Bernie threatens to beat the kids until they crap their pants. That's comedy.

Quantum Leap: Wouldn't it be awesome if Sam Beckett quantum leaped, face-first, straight into a woman's crotch? But then he realized it wasn't a woman at all? It was Al!

Barney Miller: After watching this show, I thought jail looked like fun, so I decided to rob a convenience store. Turns out real prison has a lot less hijinks and a lot more unprovoked shower-room shiv attacks.

Baywatch: Oh, God. Ever watch this show in slow motion with your hand down your pants? It's a great way to kill an afternoon.

Xena: Warrior Princess: I'm not gay or anything, but Lucy Lawless is, hands-down, the hottest guy on television.

Well, that's pretty much it. Sit, Ubu, sit! Good dog!

WHATEVER HAPPENED TO READING?
(A QUICK PLEA TO OUR NATION'S YOUTH)

GUYS, A WELL-ROUNDED MAN is a well-read man. Please, pick up a book (in addition to this one). And I'm not talking about *Harry Potter*, *The South Beach Diet*, or *Confessions of an Heiress*. I'm talking about *A Brief History of Time*, *Slaughterhouse-Five*, or even *My Life*, the Bill Clinton autobiography. Sure, he's a chubby chaser, but he's also a Rhodes scholar and, according to Mort Goldman, a great friend to Israel.

SHOW BiZ STORY

WHiLE TAPiNG our PTV sitcom, *Cheeky Bastard*, Stewie and I learned a lot about the politics of running and producing a television show. For instance, when casting our next-door neighbor, Stewie desperately wanted to use Josh Duhamel, but I preferred Donald Sutherland. Peter, though, who was the president of the network, was adamant that we use Joe Piscopo (I think they had a talent-holding deal with him or something). Ultimately, we went with Piscopo, and, don't get me wrong, he was great, but I can't help but wonder if Sutherland would have brought a little more depth to the role.

CHEEKY BASTARD

73

"You're really gonna sit there with a straight face and tell me a flat tax doesn't favor the wealthy?"

"oh, please, Peter, your excuses are lamer than FDR's legs. (everyONE gasps) Too soon?"

Politics

(The Only Bush I Trust Is Julianne Moore's in *Short Cuts*)

Sir, there's a disaster in New orleans.

Go away. I'm reading *Superfudge.*

By the time this book is published, George W. Bush will probably have this country buried underneath a tidal wave and twenty feet of rubble. But on the off chance that this has not occurred, here are some of my personal thoughts, which in no way reflect the views of Twentieth Century Fox, News Corp., or any of its subsidiaries (especially the news department).

75

GEORGE BUSH IS DRINKING AGAIN
(TRUST ME. I KNOW THE SIGNS.)

SHOWING UP LATE FOR WORK. There were Canadian Mounties who got to Katrina before Bush and the National Guard. And I know the president isn't big on geography or "book learnin'," but I can tell you that Canada is pretty far away from Louisiana.

SLURRED AND CONFUSED SPEECH. How about this one from September 2002: "There's an old saying in Tennessee—I know it's in Texas, probably in Tennessee —that says, fool me once—shame on—shame on you. You fool me, you can't get fooled again." Uh . . . what?

RUNNING UP TABS THAT YOU CAN'T PAY. According to U.S. Government estimates, by the end of this administration, the national debt will have risen from roughly $5.7 trillion to nearly $10 trillion. Well, that's even bigger than Norm Peterson's bar tab at Cheers!

PICKING FIGHTS WITH PEOPLE WHO HAVEN'T ATTACKED YOU. It turns out Iraq had very little, if anything, to do with Al Qaeda or 9/11, and they didn't have any weapons of mass destruction. But that didn't stop Bush from bombing the country halfway back to the Stone Age. **Somebody call a bouncer!**

POOR JOB PERFORMANCE. According to an independent historical research committee (myself and my cousin Jasper), George W. Bush is the third worst president in U.S. history, behind William Henry Harrison, who caught pneumonia during his inaugural address and died a month later, and Warren G. Harding, who ate puppies.

GUEST ESSAY: Peter

YOU KNOW WHAT REALLY GRINDS MY GEARS?

You know what really grinds my gears? The Supreme Court. With their fancy robes, and their gold-plated gavels and their Ruth Bader Ginsburgs . . . sittin' up there on their high horses, judging me, telling me I can't pray in school or tap my neighbors' phone lines. **Who gave them the right? Oh, the Constitution? Well, screw the Constitution, too!**

Another thing that grinds my gears is the Senate Subcommittee on Agriculture, Rural Development, and Related Agencies. There's already a Senate Agriculture Subcommittee on Forestry, Conservation, and Rural Revitalization! You guys are just making up jobs!

Another thing that grinds my gears is Uncle Sam. Who the heck do you think you're pointing at? Me? How come? Because I steal cable? Because I don't pay my taxes on time? Because I use my city-issued recycling bin as an emergency outdoor toilet? Well, you know what? Whenever you point at somebody, you got four fingers pointing right back at you. That's right. What kind of uncle are you anyway? You never bought me a birthday present. You never gave me a noogie. And I'll bet if we did a DNA test, we'd find that you're not related to me at all, but just some creepy old man in a weird jacket and top hat who's trying to get me to join the army!

You know what else grinds my gears? Habeas corpus. It's completely unfair and outdated, and I don't know why we don't overhaul the entire system completely. It's really just a travesty of justice, and, uh . . . okay, I've gotta level with you—I have no clue what habeas corpus is. But the editor said I needed four things that grind my gears, and, well, *Highway to Heaven* was on TV Land, and I find Michael Landon's hair inspirational. So, yeah . . .

And that, readers, is what grinds my gears. Brian?

WHY I DRIVE A PRIUS

YOU MAY HAVE NOTICED that I drive a hybrid car—a Prius, to be exact. And I know what you're thinking: "Brian, you're a big Hollywood star. You can afford any car you want. Plus, you have a penis that retracts into your body when you stand up. You should buy a Lamborghini."

> As a nonhuman animal, I am ultrasensitive to man's exploitation of the environment.

All valid points, but as a nonhuman animal, I am ultrasensitive to man's exploitation of the environment. As a dog, I am especially sensitive to natural resources being abused as fuel, **‹ Believe it or not, in some parts of the world, such as Alaska and Greenland, my relatives are still used to pull sleds. ›** The Prius, on the other hand, by being extremely fuel efficient and emitting fewer pollutants than other cars, can help lower our reliance on oil (which might also save us half a dozen wars in a certain desert on the other side of the world) and can help slow down global warming (which, despite President Bush's extreme faith, still exists).

Plus, hybrid cars are trendy. In addition to myself, Larry David, Leonardo DiCaprio, Cameron Diaz, Will Ferrell, Salma Hayek, and Rory Gilmore all drive Priuses. DiCaprio in particular uses his to troll Sunset Strip with David Blaine and Lukas Haas. But don't worry, girls! They're just a coupla guys hanging out! And someday Leo's gonna settle down and marry every single one of you!

HOW ABOUT A LITTLE LESS QUESTIONS AND A LITTLE MORE SHUT THE HELL UP?

POLITICO STORY

IT'S ALWAYS EMBARRASSING when you get caught licking your testicles. One time, I was at a cocktail party fund-raiser for the Democratic Congressional Campaign Committee, and I realized I hadn't cleaned my undercarriage before I left home. Well, I figured nobody would wander into the host's laundry room during the party, but, wouldn't you know it, Senator Chuck Schumer was having a little trouble finding the restroom, and he walked in on me midlick. There was an awkward kind of "Hey, this isn't the bathroom" moment, which I tried to defuse with a joke about me looking for WMDs in my crotch. But Senator Schumer didn't laugh, and I haven't been invited back to a DCCC event since.

"My day? 'Un-freakin'-believable.' First-first we nailed this bastard who had the gall to hide his stuff in his daughter's doll. Her doll, for God's sake. Where's the line anymore? Well, I got news for you: it's-it's-it's-it's-it's not even on the radar screen!"

The Workforce
(Why I'd Rather Chew on My Crotch and Chase Birds)

Let's face it, the life of your average working man is pretty thankless. You toil for fourteen hours a day, largely for the benefit of the richest 1 percent of the population, and then you come home to crap like *The War at Home* and *Skating with Celebrities*.

My advice to you young people is either **marry rich,** like Kevin Federline or Anna Nicole Smith (granted, not your ideal role models, but in terms of amassing a great deal of wealth with only a tiny drop of talent, they're pretty damn efficient); **invent something useful,** like the guy who created AstroTurf (I hear he lives in a mansion made of diamonds and wipes his ass with thousand-dollar bills); or **go into show business,** because, let's be honest, what they do isn't real work. That's why celebrities are always getting into trouble with the law, abusing drugs, and stealing one another's spouses. They have nothing better to do.

Or, if you're a dog like me (or a hamster, a cat, or Luke Perry's pig), you can **find an amenable family and mooch off of them** while lying around the house all day, sipping martinis, reading the *New York Times*, and half-heartedly outlining your novel.

VARIOUS JOBS

I HAVE, though, in the past, had several thankless workaday jobs:

HUMMER SALESMAN: This occupation was soul crushing (I told you, I drive a Prius) as well as unrewarding. Also, my boss was Patty Tanninger, who is so unbelievably annoying. I mean, the guy only has one joke, and it's not even that funny. Don't worry, though—we're gonna kill him off this coming season.

CASHSCAM EMPLOYEE: Working under Stewie was humiliating. And I'm not even sure what we did. The only instruction he ever gave me was, "You pick up that phone and you sell, sell, sell!" Plus, he told me I have smelly dog-farts, which, however true, was still hurtful.

DRUG-SNIFFING POLICE DOG: This job was actually great. I put criminals behind bars, and I really got to feel like I was part of a team. Unfortunately, it turns out I have, um, a bit of an addictive personality, and I got hooked on blow (the same thing happened to Tackleberry in *Police Academy 4*).

ESSAYIST FOR *THE NEW YORKER*: This was my dream job . . . before I knew what I really wanted. The contributors at *The New Yorker* were all stuck-up, brandy-swilling, elitist intellectuals, and . . . Aw, who am I kidding?

The days of decency and virtue are gone, honey. Bam! freakin' evaporated like a dingy, stinkin' mud puddle.

I loved it there! It was the best job I ever had! Please, Mr. Shepherdson, take me back! At least let me draw an "illustrated laughing square"!

PORNOGRAPHIC FILM DIRECTOR: This, too, was not such a bad gig. And I was good at it. I even won a Woody award, the only trophy so graphic, you can't show it

So, you wanna party or what?

on TV. (I'll give you a hint: when George Michael comes over, I have to hide it.) But, ultimately, the job made me feel dirty. Like Peter, when he was a transvestite prostitute.

SUBSTITUTE TEACHER: Is there a more thankless job in the entire world? There wasn't a single student in my remedial English class who wasn't packing heat, running numbers, or tripping balls. One kid actually wore a diaper. The only plus side was that it was a great place to score a little weed. Oops, just got another note from my editor: apparently, I don't use drugs, I've never used drugs, and any evidence to the contrary is purely the result of "extreme dehydration."

WHAT DO I DO ALL DAY?

YOU CAN SEE WHY I'd rather chew on my crotch and chase birds. In fact, a lot of fans have expressed curiosity about what I do all day. Well, here it is, an average day in the life of Brian Griffin:

8:45 A.m.: Wake up, have a cup of coffee, read the paper.

9:06 A.m.: Take a dump in the front yard.

9:41 A.m.: Watch last night's *Charlie Rose*. Then check the Internet to see who's going to be on the show tonight. E-mail questions pertaining to his or her area of expertise.

10:56 A.m.: Look through Lois's underwear drawer. (Don't you judge me!)

11:08 A.m.: "Alone time" in the bathroom.

12:01 P.m.: Work on my novel for about an hour. I'm still at the outline stage, but it's only been three years.

Ooh, I have so much to do today.

1:15 P.m.: Lunchtime. Most days, I'll go with the liquid lunch of a martini and a handful of olives. Sometimes I'll throw in a Cobb salad.

2:38 P.m.: Run a few errands. Buy a pack of smokes, drop off a Netflix package, piss on a parking meter.

5:05 P.m.: Hit the park with Peter and get some exercise. We usually just toss around the Frisbee, but sometimes we'll join Tricia Takanawa for some tai chi.

5:58 P.m.: Happy hour. Another few martinis at the Drunken Clam or in front of the TV. Sometimes we'll see how many toothpicks we can stab into Joe's legs before he notices. On a good day, we'll get about fifteen or twenty before Cleveland starts to giggle.

7:18 P.m.: Dinnertime. By now I have a pretty good buzz going. I just gotta avoid watching Meg chew, so I don't hurl my casserole.

8:45 P.m.: Dig up trinkets in the backyard. Bury them again.

9:52 P.m.: Curl up at the foot of Peter and Lois's bed. This is actually my favorite part of the day. The bed is warm and toasty, and I get to hang out with some of my favorite people.

10:15 P.m.: Get kicked out because the bastards want to "make bacon."

10:18 P.m.: Listen at the door for a few minutes.

10:26 P.m.: Switch to hard stuff (either Jack Daniel's or Glenfiddich) and pop in an old movie.

11:41 P.m.: Make a drunken phone call to an old girlfriend.

12:13 A.m.: Cry myself to sleep.

8:45 Am: Wake up, take an aspirin, and do it all over again.

WORKING SCHLUB STORY

WHEN I WORKED AT *THE NEW YORKER* (for all of three hours), my boss, Wellesley Shepherdson, explained to me that they had no toilets in the building because nobody at *The New Yorker* had an anus. Curious, I did some research to see how they were able to digest and excrete their food without anal canals. This is what I found out:

The employees at *The New Yorker* ingest food just like the rest of us: they chew it in their mouths, swallow it down their esophagi, and begin digesting it in their stomachs. This, however, is where the similarities end. Before the half-digested food hits their small intestines, the ghost of John Cheever magically appears, whisks it away, and deposits it in Newark, New Jersey.

THIS NEXT ONE YOU <u>CAN</u> BLAME ON THE DOG.

THAT FEELS
SO GOOD!!
THAT FEELS SO GOOD!
THAT FEELS SO GOOD!
THAT FEELS SO GOOD!
THAT FEELS SO GOOD!
THAT FEELS SO GOOD!
THAT FEELS SO GOOD!

Chapt

"That man has got magic fingers. He found this one spot behind my ear, forget about it, I thought my leg was never gonna stop."

"You know, if dogs aren't supposed to eat dental floss out of the garbage, why do they make it mint flavored?"

A Dog's Life

(Advantages and Drawbacks to Being a Four-legged Mammal)

So...it's a show about three hookers and their mom?

Being a man means having to deal with life's ups and downs. Sure, you can pee standing up, and you don't have to incubate and birth your young, but you also can't teach kindergarten or fully appreciate *Sex and the City*.

Being a dog also has its advantages and its drawbacks. Here are my thoughts (and my gay cousin Jasper's) on the subject.

YOU WOULD IF YOU COULD
(TOP FIVE ADVANTAGES TO BEING A DOG)

5. CAN SHAKE MYSELF DRY. Ever get out of the shower, and you're like, "Damn it, I forgot to bring a towel," and then you have to make a wet, naked beeline to your bedroom? Not me.

4. CAN LICK MY OWN CROTCH. I usually like to pretend I'm Jessica Alba.

3. THERE'S A SPOT ON MY RIB CAGE WHERE, IF YOU SCRATCH IT, MY LEG SHAKES UNCONTROLLABLY AND I'M IN ECSTASY FOR ABOUT FORTY-FIVE MINUTES. And as you might imagine, it's much easier to convince a girl to scratch your rib cage than certain other places.

2. CAN CATCH A FRISBEE IN MY MOUTH. It hurts, and my dentist keeps telling me not to do it, but it's a big hit at parties.

1. CAN LICK MY OWN CROTCH. I know I put it on here twice, but this time I'm pretending I'm Markie Post.

MR. HOOVER
(TOP FIVE DRAWBACKS TO BEING A DOG)

5. FEAR OF THE VACUUM CLEANER. I know it's irrational, and I know the damn thing can't really hurt me, but it's so F-ing loud! It scares the piss out of me! And Lois knows it, too. She calls it "Mr. Hoover" and brings it out whenever she wants to strong-arm me into doing something.

4. LACK OF PRESTIGE. But I guess that comes with the territory when you're afraid of household appliances.

95

3. SHOCKING DOG COLLARS. Is this really necessary? You can't just tell us, "Please don't go into the living room"? You really need to resort to Dick Cheney–Abu Ghraib prison tactics?

2. LIPSTICK PENIS. As Stewie enjoys pointing out, when I stand, my penis retracts into my abdomen, like a cylinder of lipstick that is being rolled back into its tube. Plus, the normal size of a tube of lipstick is, well . . . let's just say, Ron Jeremy doesn't have anything to worry about.

1. I CAN DIE FROM EATING CHOCOLATE. That's right. Just like the nerdy kid from your elementary school class who was deathly allergic to everything, I can't eat chocolate without slipping into a coma. And I hear it's pretty good. I mean, Kirstie Alley gave up sleep, men, and her career for it.

GUEST ESSAY: Jasper

"BEING A GAY CANINE IS FABULOUS!"

Hi, kids! Jasper, Brian's straight as a zig-zag cousin, here to tell you why being a gay canine is fabulous!

First of all, ever scratch your own ear with your foot while getting freaky with a skinny, hairless Filipino boy on your kitchen floor? Didn't think so, because you're not a dog, so you can't scratch your ear with your foot! And you're not gay, so you probably have hoo-hoo intercourse! Ewww! Gag me with a cucumber!

Second, gay canines are every-where! Even some of the most famous dogs in the world are gay. Spuds MacKen-zie? Big butch. Taco Bell Chihuahua? Chorizo

queen. Snoopy? Let's just say he wasn't above tempting Woodstock by putting a little birdseed on his Kibbles 'n Bits. Ooo! I'm terrible! Stick a lightbulb in me, I'm done!

Finally, **the gay canine lifestyle is to die for! I shake my moneymaker all day long, teaching dance classes at Club Med with a handful (and I do mean handful!) of sweaty young studs in Speedo bathing suits.**

Then I take a shower (make it a cold one, please!) and get all dolled up for the nightlife. And you *know* gay clubs are the hottest clubs. With the pounding beats and the fast tempos . . . oh, and the music's pretty good, too! Ooo! Score another one for me! I'm flaming (and my jokes aren't bad, either)! Finally, at about 4:00 A.M., I limp home and snuggle with Ricardo, my little Asian pincushion. I know, I'm a rice queen. Sue me.

So, in conclusion, if you're a dog, go gay. You haven't enjoyed a liver treat until you've eaten it off a shaved and oiled chest. Oh, and if you're human, give a dog a bone. You won't regret it!

Toodles (show me your noodles)!

Jasper

Note: Neither HarperCollins Publishers, Twentieth Century Fox Television, nor Fox Broadcasting Company condones bestiality, the insertion of lightbulbs into bodily orifices, or getting freaky with hairless, skinny Filipino boys on your kitchen floor.

DOG STORY

HAVE YOU EVER BEEN TO THE POUND?

I got thrown in there a while back, when (a little edgy from living on the streets) I bit a pedestrian. Well, let me tell you, I was in there long enough to know that I never wanna go back. There were pit bulls, Rottweilers, Dobermans, and one really vicious toy poodle who'd escaped from a cosmetics testing facility. We called him Toy George, but not to his face because he'd gnaw your ear right off. My point is, to any puppies out there who might be reading this, stay off the streets because there's nothing like waking up with a Doberman's hot breath on the back of your neck to scare you straight.

Oh, look, a tasty little baby.

lany
Miscellany

(Or Various Thoughts from a Bar Stool at the Drunken Clam, Circa 2:00 A.M.)

The Drunken Clam

KiDS
(AND WHY THEY CREEP THE HELL OUT OF ME)

DON'T GET ME WRONG— I'd love to be a father someday, and I'm sure I'll care for my offspring very much, but other people's children just creep the living hell out of me.

First of all, the crying drives me nuts. What are you crying about? I can't understand you, because you're just wailing uncontrollably and turning red and not giving me words! Oh, and by the way, your screeching is making my brain boil, and I'm about to drive an ice pick through my temple, but, yeah, you're very cute when you're sleeping.

The other thing is the sticky hands. Why are they sticky? Are they jamming them in their mouths? I sure hope so, because some of the other options are much less appealing. Sure, lady, it's very sweet that your kid wants to hand me a Cheerio, but why do his hands smell like old cheese?

I guess the only thing worse than someone else's baby is someone else's slightly effeminate, homicidal baby bent on world domination. "Damn us all"? Come on, kid. You smell like crap. Get your own house in order before you start trying to take over the planet. (I kid Stewie, of course. He knows that I wish him and whatever versatile-top bear-butch he ends up with all the happiness in the world.)

I'm a friendly dog, but if your kid touches me with his booger hands, things could get ugly.

THE MYTH THAT i DON'T LiKE BLACK PEOPLE

i'M GLAD TO HAVE THE OPPORTUNiTY to clear up this popular misconception, once and for all. You see, it all started when I barked rather violently at Dr. Diddy, our African American record producer, a few dozen times. And I just

NATE GRIFFIN

want to say, that (a) it was totally involuntary and I have no idea what came over me, and (b) it's a relic from my father's generation that, quite frankly, I'm ashamed of.

It is *so* not me. I vote Democrat, I love *Benson*, and I wasn't really that pissed about the O.J. verdict. Well, I was pissed, but it's because he's rich, not because he's black.

Also, would I have dated Shauna Parks if I didn't like black people? And I know what you're gonna say: "Thomas Jefferson fell in love with and sired several children with an African American woman, but he still had slaves." Well, I *don't* have slaves. And **as I've said before, if I was offered a slave I'd say no.**

Also, I'm a staunch supporter of affirmative action. And if that means that when Meg graduates from high school she doesn't get into an Ivy League college

because an African American student is admitted ahead of her, that's fine. It's worth it, because black Americans had to suffer through hundreds of years of slavery, and even today they face greater socioeconomic hurdles than their white counterparts. I— I'm sorry . . . I just have to stop for a second here. I thought I could get through this without cracking up, but the idea of Meg even *applying* to an Ivy League school

is just hilarious to me. I mean, she couldn't even hack it at Cornell. Mike Tyson would have a better chance or getting into Harvard than Meg. And I'm not saying that because he's black. I'm saying that because he's stupid, and he threatens to rape people and eat their babies.

MY NOVEL

YEAH, I KNOW IT'S REAL FUNNY when Stewie pokes fun at me for not having made much progress on my novel. "How you coming on that novel you working on? Hmm? Got a big, uh, big stack of papers there? Got a nice little, nice little story you working on there? Your big novel you've been working on for three years? Hmm?" But the truth is, I'm reconceiving the entire piece right now. I gave the first hundred pages or so to a few of my more literary-type friends

< Cleveland chose not to read it because it was "white literature," and Peter lost interest after twenty pages because "there were no boobs">

and, for the most part, they agreed that while the protagonist could be a little more "likable," there was a lot of good material in there.

I have to admit that because the main character is loosely based on myself, it was a little painful to hear that he was "unlikable." But when you're a writer, sometimes you have to check your feelings at the door. Either that or drink until you can't remember what you felt in the first place. At least, that's what Hemingway did. And he was a modern master.

STEWIE
Maybe your main character gets into a relationship? Suffers a little heartbreak? Something like, uh, what you've just been through? Draw from, uh, real-life experiences? Little, uh, little heartbreak, you know, work it into the story? Make those characters a little more three-dimensional? A little, uh, richer experience for the reader? Make those second hundred pages really keep the reader guessing what's going to happen?

A FINAL WORD ON THE LOST ART OF BEING A MAN

WHEN THE FOLKS at HarperCollins first approached me about writing this book, I said no. I was hurt and quite frankly a little bitter that they'd asked Stewie to write a book first. (I mean, what did that pompous little Baby Hyde Pierce know that I didn't?) But after the initial pain subsided, I said yes. Because men in the twenty-first century have gone soft. And they need somebody to remind them how to be real men. In this case, it's a dog.

Frank Sinatra once said, "You gotta love livin', baby, 'cause dyin' is a pain in the ass!" And he was right. You can follow every bit of advice in this book, but if you don't have a certain zest for life, a joie de vivre, a little snap in your tongue when you lick your nads, then what's it all worth? Nothing. So, get out there and pee on a fire hydrant, get tossed out of a bar, sing a swingin' tune, punch a guy out, give a chorus girl your room number, read a book with no pictures, catch a Frisbee in your mouth, buy a round of beers for a crowded pub, wake up on a tramp steamer headed to Portugal, live life to the fullest, drink like Gleason, dress like Bogart, fight like Hemingway, and love like Jack Kennedy.

Good luck, and as Frank used to say, "Here's to the confusion of our enemies!"

—B. G.

> Drink like Gleason, dress like Bogart, fight like Hemingway, and love like Jack Kennedy.

ACKNOWLEDGMENTS

This book would not be possible without the guidance and support of Debbie Olshan, and the creativity and keen editorial eyes of Casey Kait and Hope Innelli. In addition, the counsel provided by Steve Callaghan and David Goodman was invaluable and much appreciated. And finally, this book (along with Brian Griffin and the entire town of Quahog) would not even exist without Seth MacFarlane, a great boss, a great friend, and the most talented guy I've ever met.

—A. G.

Nah, that's cool. No need to thank me. I'm just a dog. I don't even have a soul.

—B. G.

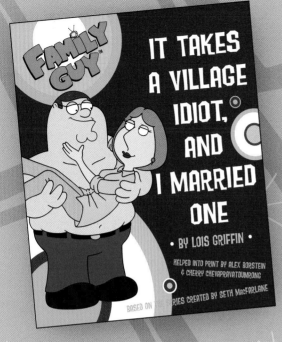

IT TAKES A VILLAGE IDIOT, AND I MARRIED ONE

COMING SOON!

After unseating incumbent Adam West, who departs office under a cloud of scandal, Lois Griffin not only becomes Quahog's first female mayor, she also joins the ranks of controversial public figures who serve and tell-all in this dishy, no-holds-barred memoir, complete with tributes from family, friends and valued constituents! Available in bookstores April 2007.

The Stewie Griffin SCHOOL OF HARD KNOCKS Grad Pad

ISBN 0-06-114869-5

Part scrapbook, part memory album, part down-and-dirty slam book, this is the place for aspiring and recent grads to record the most memorable events of their school careers. With lots of room for them and their peeps to enter photos, musings, memories and pithy one-liners, this book includes hilarious accounts of the Griffin clan's own most embarrassing, degrading and undignified moments, too!

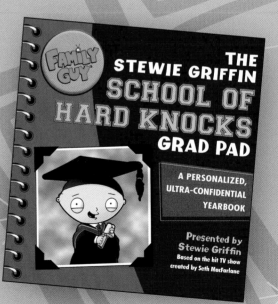

Visit www.AuthorTracker.com
for exclusive information on your favorite HarperCollins authors.

Available wherever books are sold, or call 1-800-331-3761 to order.